EDU   ERVICE

FIND YOUR TALENT
TAKE GREAT PHOTOS!

Adam Sutherland

W
FRANKLIN WATTS
LONDON • SYDNEY

First published in 2012 by Franklin Watts

Copyright © 2012 Arcturus Publishing Limited

Franklin Watts
338 Euston Road
London NW1 3BH

Franklin Watts Australia
Level 17/207 Kent Street, Sydney NSW 2000

Produced by Arcturus Publishing Limited,
26/27 Bickels Yard, 151-153 Bermondsey Street, London SE1 3HA

Text: Adam Sutherland
Editors: Joe Harris and Sarah Eason
Design: Paul Myerscough
Cover design: Akihiro Nakayama

Picture credits:
Cover images: Shutterstock: Conrado bc, Dinga br, Pichugin Dmitry bl, EpicStockMedia tl, Lakov Filimonov ccl, JCJG Photography tr, Mikeledray ccr, Pavelk ct, Andrey Shadrin tc, Elena Yakusheva cr, Zulufoto cl.
Interior images: Dreamstime: Heidi Dp 19bl, Nikolay Mamluke 25br, Anatoliy Smirnov 3tl, 18bl, Hongqi Zhang 9bl; Getty: AFP 11bl; Serif (Europe) Ltd: 13tr, 26–27tc; Shutterstock: Yuri Arcurs 17b, Noam Armonn 3bl, 22b, Basel101658 8bl, Dhoxax 12–13c, Dinga 14br, Djgis 14–15bc, Lane V. Erickson 7tr, Daria Filimonova 27br, Filip Fuxa 4–5tc, Alvin Ganesh 4cr, Jarp2 14bl, Aaron Kohr 21cl, Yan Lev 6–7b, Littleny 24–25bc, Artem Loskutnikov 27cl, Luxorphoto 26bl, Marietjie 23bl, Ilja Mašík 20–21c, Tatiana Morozova 16tr, Antonio Jorge Nunes 11tl, Christopher Edwin Nuzzaco 8tr, Pashabo 6bl, Pavelk 01, Valerie Potapova 5bl, Chen Wei Seng 21tl, Nickolay Stanev 28–29tc, Stacie Stauff Smith Photography 29tr, Eduard Titov 19br, USBFCO 23tr, Vesilvio 10tr, Vipflash 13br, OtnaYdur 24bl, Zurijeta 16cr.

A CIP catalogue record for this book is available from the British Library.

Dewey Decimal Classification Number 771-dc23

ISBN-13: 978 1 4451 1014 1

Printed in China

Franklin Watts is a division of Hachette Children's Books, an Hachette UK company.
www.hachette.co.uk

SL002142EN
Supplier 03 Date 0412 Print run 1452

CONTENTS

FIND YOUR TALENT!

A great sunset deserves a great picture – and we'll show you how.

To take great photographs, you need a top-of-the-range camera, a massive zoom lens and other expensive kit, right? Wrong! Digital photography is easy, instant fun. Everyone can take amazing pictures just by following a few simple rules.

Not on film! Digital cameras take photos without film and save them as files on your camera's memory. You can see your pictures straight away and transfer, or download, the best ones onto a computer. Digital pictures are made up of millions of tiny squares called pixels, which are almost invisible but combine to make a photograph. The more pixels your camera puts into each photo, the better the resolution.

Higher means bigger The higher a photograph's resolution, the bigger you can enlarge or print it. To take photographs at a high resolution, you need a camera with more than five million pixels – or up to 10 or 12 million, if possible. Cameras with fewer pixels can still take great shots, but you will be more limited in what you can do with the picture afterwards.

Digital cameras are ready to shoot – anytime, anywhere!

INSIDE STORY: THE ORIGINAL PHOTOJOURNALIST

French photographer Henri Cartier-Bresson invented photojournalism. Instead of taking pictures of people in photographic studios dressed up and looking their best, he took pictures in the street of people going about their daily lives. He once said, 'Your first 10,000 photographs are your worst.' Get out there and shoot, make mistakes and learn from them!

Today, you can even use your mobile phone to take memorable holiday snaps – now there's no excuse!

Let's go! In this book, we will explain how to take brilliant photos with any kind of digital camera, from mobile phones and digital music players to SLR cameras. We will be looking at when to take your picture, what to include in your photos, and how to get the best out of snapping your friends, pets, landscapes and sports. Try out all the tips, work out what all your camera's buttons do, and start taking amazing digital photos!

PICK THE MOMENT

How do you know when to take a picture? This is a big question, but luckily there is more than one answer!

Ready to shoot! To capture the perfect shot, look for the decisive moment – for example when a bird spreads its wings, when your granddad yawns or when your little sister drops her ice cream on the floor. Shoot a second too early or a second too late, and you may miss the best shot. Be ready for the crucial moment: take your camera wherever you go, and have it in your hand, ready to shoot. Think about what shot you want to take. This will save you time when a great picture presents itself.

All in the timing Some photos can be taken only at a specific moment, but others benefit from being taken at different times of the day. Long shadows in the early morning and late afternoon can make pictures look more dramatic than shots taken at midday when shadows are short. Similarly, the sun directly overhead can create unflattering shadows on people's faces, and can cause them to squint if they are looking into the sun. Experiment with shooting at different times of day, and see for yourself what works best.

Waiting for the perfect moment to shoot can takes patience, but it's worth it.

GO FOR IT: TIMING

Choosing the right time of day to take a picture can be the key to success:

- Find a subject. It could be a tree, a flower or a landmark.
- Take a picture of the subject first thing in the morning, at midday and in the late afternoon and compare the pictures.
- You will see long shadows at the start and end of the day. Include these in your picture for a more dramatic shot.

Using your brain as well as your camera will produce eye-catching results.

Remember your special events with well-composed and well-planned pictures.

EARLY DAYS: Camera apps

Apps such as *Instagram* make it easy to take stunning, vintage-looking pictures on an iPhone or Android phone. Pop singer Justin Bieber popularised *Instagram* when he tweeted one of its pictures – soon 50 people per minute were joining the service. Today, it has 10 million users.

TAKING GREAT PHOTOS

Even if you just want to take pictures of your friends, these photos can be improved if you spend some time planning the composition of your photo.

A portrait can be made more striking by positioning the subject away from the centre.

Setting it up Composition means how your photograph looks – where the person in the picture is standing and what is going on in the background. Most people's first thought will probably be to position the subject right in the middle of the shot. However, if you look at some of the best professional photographs, you will see that the subject is often positioned to one side. This is called the rule of thirds, because placing the subject along the outer third of a picture often produces the best results.

Here, the horizon and the tree meet on one of the imaginary 'rule of thirds' lines.

Less is more Once you have positioned your subject, you need to think about the background of your shot. The less distracting the background, the better your picture will be. If you are shooting indoors, avoid patterned wallpaper or eye-catching posters. Tidying away clutter always helps!

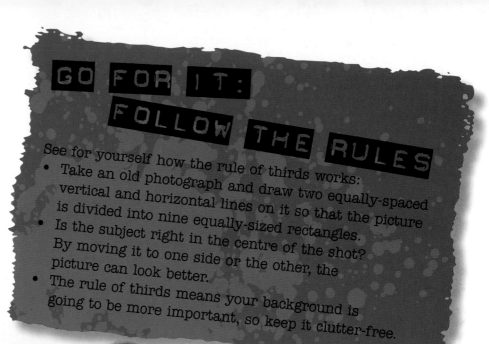

GO FOR IT: FOLLOW THE RULES

See for yourself how the rule of thirds works:
- Take an old photograph and draw two equally-spaced vertical and horizontal lines on it so that the picture is divided into nine equally-sized rectangles.
- Is the subject right in the centre of the shot? By moving it to one side or the other, the picture can look better.
- The rule of thirds means your background is going to be more important, so keep it clutter-free.

Standing friends one in front of the other adds interest to an otherwise standard composition.

INSIDE STORY: JOHN RANKIN WADDELL

Celebrity photographer Rankin is world-famous for his eye-catching portraits of pop stars and Hollywood actors. He says, 'Photographs are a kind of fantasy of how the photographer sees the subject. We use lighting and backgrounds... to create an image that, hopefully, tells you something about that person.'

SHARP AND CLEAR

Most cameras have focus and zoom functions. But what are they and how can you use them to take better pictures? Check the functions available for your camera in your manual, then follow this guide.

Fuzz alert! The autofocus function is programmed to focus on what is in the centre of your picture, to ensure that it is not blurred. If your subject is to one side, you could easily take a great shot of the wall and a fuzzy picture of your friend!

Stop the fuzz! Many cameras have a focus lock. If your camera has this, centre on the subject and press the shutter release button halfway down. This tells the camera where you want it to focus. Now frame the picture and take the shot.

Here, a zoom lens creates an unusual and amusing portrait.

INSIDE STORY: SLINKACHU

London street artist Slinkachu uses his camera's zoom lens to maximum effect! Slinkachu – real name unknown – creates art using tiny, toy models of people (the kind that are used with model train sets). He arranges them on the street – waiting for a model bus, or rowing a model boat through a puddle – and photographs them as if they are part of a normal, full-size world. His art is so small that pedestrians often don't realise they are walking past pieces of art, but the photographs sell for thousands of pounds!

Zoom in By adjusting the zoom setting on your camera lens, you can bring a subject closer or move it further away. If you adjust the lens to both a zoom and wide setting (wide zoom setting), the camera will take a wide shot of something far away. This is good for taking pictures of mountains in the distance, for example, as the zoom brings them closer, while the wide angle keeps the mountains in shot.

Short and wide If you are taking a picture of a few friends, avoid the wide zoom – it fits everyone in, but makes them look shorter and wider. Instead, step back and zoom in using the tele zoom. The tele zoom brings you closer to your subject, but crops out more of the background.

Slinkachu blurs fantasy and reality with the clever positioning of toys in his photographs.

GO FOR IT: ZOOM IT

Work out how to use your zoom and wide lens settings, then try the following:

- Take pictures of a group of friends with your zoom setting.
- Take the same picture with the wide zoom setting.
- What happens to the subjects of each picture?
- What happens to the background of each picture?
- Which shots look the best?

LIGHT IT UP

If you are taking pictures indoors or in the evening, a camera flash can help to provide enough light for you to take good quality shots. Choosing when to use your flash – and when not to use it – can also improve your pictures.

Fooling the flash A standard camera flash has a range of two to three metres, so if you want to shoot a sunset, or a band on stage it will not help. Instead, switch off the flash, and rely on whatever lighting is available.

Speedy shutters On some cameras, you will be able to adjust the camera's shutter speed. This means lengthening the time that the camera's shutter stays open in order to allow as much light into the camera as possible. You can tell a slow shutter speed by the length of time between the clicks of the shutter opening and closing. Look at your camera manual to find out how to adjust your shutter speed time.

By adjusting your camera's shutter speed, you can achieve incredibly atmospheric shots.

GO FOR IT: STAYING SHARP

To take a shot that's in focus, keep your camera very steady:

- Use a tripod to prevent camera shake. A wall, table or the branch of a tree can all provide good support.
- Keep your arms tucked in close to your body and plant your feet shoulder-width apart. Try not to move!

Angry eyes! Red-eye describes the annoying red dots that are seen in some people's eyes in pictures taken with a flash. The red-eye reduction setting will trigger a bright light, or series of lights, before the flash actually goes off. These lights cause the subject's pupils to dilate before the shot is taken, reducing red-eye.

Red-eye reduction is a common setting on most digital cameras. Bye bye to angry red eyes!

Pop music innovator and now creative director of Polaroid, Lady Gaga is bringing bright ideas to the camera company.

INSIDE STORY: LADY GAGA

Singer Lady Gaga is the creative director of camera company Polaroid. In 2011, Polaroid launched the singer's first invention: camera glasses. The stylish pair of shades can take pictures, and can also be used to watch videos or to share photos with friends. 'I brought my love of fashion, technology and obsession with the future into all of my work with Polaroid,' she says.

STILL GOT IT!

Now that you have mastered your camera and know the theory behind taking a good shot, you need to practise. It is a good idea to start with things that do not move, such as a still life scene or landscape.

Depth of field The most important thing for any kind of still life or landscape picture is to maximise your depth of field. This means to get as much of the shot in focus as possible. Setting your shutter speed to slow will achieve this effect.

GO FOR IT: LANDSCAPES

Follow these useful tips for shooting great landscapes:

- Look for something that will stand out and catch the viewer's eye – an interesting tree or an old building. This is called a focal point. Position it in the shot, paying attention to the rule of thirds (see page 8).
- If the sky is full of dramatic-looking clouds or a beautiful blue, then use it. If it is dull or overcast, keep it to a minimum.
- Use straight lines, such as a road or overhead cables, to draw people into a picture.
- Try to capture movement, such as wind in the trees, to add drama and interest to your shots.

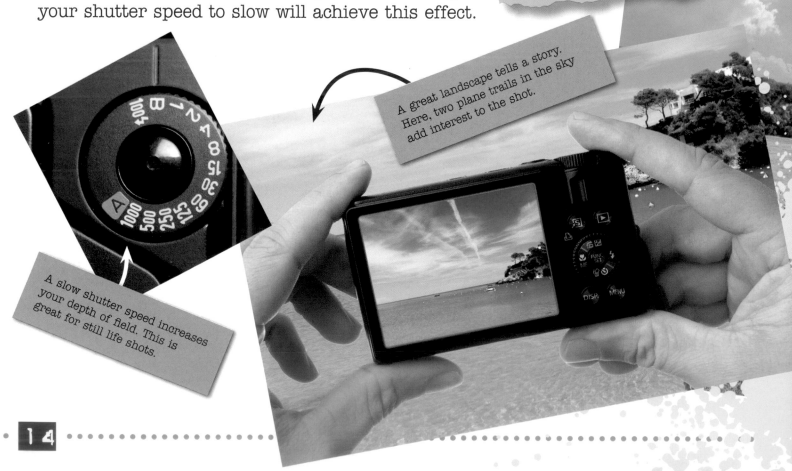

A great landscape tells a story. Here, two plane trails in the sky add interest to the shot.

A slow shutter speed increases your depth of field. This is great for still life shots.

A winding path 'leads' your viewer into this shot. The sun breaking from behind the cloud is a great bonus!

INSIDE STORY:

Charlie Waite left school and trained to be an actor. To fill in time between acting jobs, he started taking pictures of his fellow actors, and was bitten by the photography bug. He is now an award-winning landscape photographer, known for his beautifully-lit pictures. 'Light is really important,' he says. 'Clouds can completely change the light on a landscape and I often wait four or five hours to get the right shot – but it's worth it!'

The right light

Lighting is also important for still life photography. Make sure your flash is switched off or it will blow away the interesting shadows and shades of colour. Use natural light whenever possible, and use a slow shutter speed and a tripod to make sure there is no wobble.

SAY CHEESE!

Photographing people is more difficult than just shouting, 'Say cheese!' So how do you make sure you get the best shots when you are creating portraits?

A great portrait captures the essence of the person you are shooting. Eyes, smile and character are more important than backgrounds.

One at a time If you are shooting just one person, try using the portrait exposure if your camera has one. It makes the background go slightly out of focus, and brings your attention to the subject of the picture. Keep the background as simple as possible, and fill the frame with your subject.

A PRINCESS WITHOUT SHOES

INSIDE STORY:

The best portraits clearly show the subject's character. Photographer Mario Testino will always be remembered for his portraits of the late Princess Diana. 'My original idea was to photograph [her] in her tiara,' he remembers. 'But then I thought, am I interested in seeing another picture of her as a royal person, or would I rather see what she is actually about? And that's why I decided to do her without jewels, without shoes, without trimmings.'

A crowd of people Shooting a crowd of people takes perseverance! To make sure you get a good selection of shots where everyone's eyes are open, the simplest thing is to take lots of pictures. Try sitting some people down and have others standing behind them. Having heads at different heights makes your shots more interesting. Squashing everyone together a bit means you can zoom in closer, too.

Eye-catching group shots aren't easy to compose. This one, shot from above with an emphasis on fun, is a real winner.

GO FOR IT: PORTRAITS

By capturing someone's real self – not just a front they put on for the camera – you can turn a snapshot into a portrait:

- If you do not know your subject, try spending time with him or her before you shoot.
- Think about using props, such as hats, to add character.
- Direct your subject, telling him or her how to pose. Your subject does not know what you are seeing through the viewfinder, so you will need to explain.
- Keep it fun and keep talking. If your subject has difficulty posing, talk about topics other than the picture to relax him or her.

FINE-TUNING YOUR PORTRAITS

Now that you have mastered composition, it is time to turn your pictures of people into real masterpieces.

Seeing eye to eye Where you stand in relation to the subject of your photograph can make a massive difference to how good your pictures look. To get the right angle for your picture, work out the subject's eye level, and then raise or lower yourself until you are the same height. You will see the difference in your pictures.

Think about eye levels – do you need to get up high or down low for a better shot?

GO FOR IT: THINKING ON YOUR FEET

Here are some tips for getting the right angle:
- Try standing on a chair to raise yourself to the height of someone taller than you.
- Get on the ground! Shots of children playing on the floor, or an animal or person resting are best taken at eye level. You can also take overhead shots such as a passing aeroplane at this level.
- Swim for it! If you want to take fabulous underwater shots, don't be afraid to get you or your camera wet. Just make sure your camera is suitable for use in water.

MICHAEL YAMASHITA

INSIDE STORY:

Michael Yamashita has been shooting for National Geographic magazine for 30 years. He believes that great pictures come from careful planning. 'I usually have an image in my mind of what I want,' he says, 'and that takes a lot of the guesswork out of it. Occasionally, you get lucky and grab a single frame that really works, but mainly I know what I want and work hard to get it.'

Catch the moment

Pictures of your friends smiling for the camera are fine, but you will soon feel the urge to try something more adventurous! When you are out together, get into the habit of taking your camera with you, and thinking about possible shots (see pages 6–7). Also, standing back from the action and using your zoom will get you better shots. If people forget you are there, they will act much more naturally.

The casual laugh says a lot about this portrait. The uncluttered background keeps it simple, too.

Children are fascinated by the world around them – capture the concentration!

ACTION SHOTS

There are times when you will want to shoot a moving subject, such as a football game or friends running in a race. Read on to ensure you get the best action shots.

Panning For great pictures of a moving subject, you need to pan your camera. This means following the subject in the viewfinder before, during and after you take the picture. You can practise panning on passing cyclists or cars until you can match your movements to the speed of the action.

GO FOR IT: PAN FOR GOLD

Panning is tricky at first, but you can perfect it following these steps:
- Stand with your feet shoulder-width apart to keep yourself steady.
- Put your camera to your eye, then rotate at the waist 90 degrees. Keep your eye level steady, and your movement as careful and controlled as possible.
- Practise this movement without taking pictures at first.
- When you think you are steady enough, take a picture when you are halfway through the movement.

Capturing the excitement and exhilaration of action sports is a real challenge, but practice makes perfect!

Racing cars move fast, so don't expect great results every time. Persevere and keep panning.

Focus on focus If some of your images are coming out blurry, try using the focus lock technique we covered on page 10 to pre-focus on the spot you plan to shoot.

Don't forget! When you have your shutter button pressed halfway down, the focus is fixed. If your subject moves closer or further away, or you move closer or further to adjust your composition, your subject will be out of focus again. If you plan to use the zoom, do this before you lock the focus. The zoom will not work when the shutter release button is being pressed.

Here, a slower shutter speed softens the entire shot (not just the background), but still gives a real feeling of speed.

INSIDE STORY: ACTION HERO

Award-winning sports photographer Bob Martin has taken pictures at every major sporting event, including ten summer and winter Olympic Games. According to Bob, speed, anticipation and quick reactions are the key to getting great action shots. 'If you see the competitor in the viewfinder,' Bob says, 'you've missed the picture!'

PLAYING WITH ANIMALS

Whether you are taking pictures of your pet cat, or lions in a safari park, follow this simple guide and you will be taking great animal shots in no time.

Eyes are important Pay attention to the animal's eyes. Whether it is a dog or a leopard, if you do not get the eyes in focus, you will not get a good shot. Use your focus lock and be prepared to pan (see page 20) if necessary. Taking several shots of the same subject will also tip the odds in your favour of getting a standout picture.

An eye level view of your subject brings you up close and personal with your furry best friend.

GO FOR IT: SNAPPING THE FAMILY PETS

If you have a cute pet, here is how to get some great shots of them:

- Stick to natural light – flash can cause animals' pupils to go green, and also frightens them.
- Shoot from the pet's eye level (or below). By getting close to the ground, you can also show people what life looks like from down there!
- Try to show the animal's character. If you have a lazy cat, photograph it yawning. If your dog is playful, shoot him performing his favourite trick.
- Be patient – if you are prepared to spend time photographing your pet, you will take better shots.

Squirrels move fast, so be patient and try to capture a moment of stillness and anticipation.

A natural shot Using your zoom lens means you can get close to your subject without affecting its behaviour. Watch your subject for a while and take in what it is doing, and how it is moving. Anticipate what it might do next. A few minutes study could mean the difference between a good shot and a great one.

Use your zoom to enter a spider's miniature world. You'll be amazed at what you find when you zoom in.

REALY WILD PHOTOGRAPHY

INSIDE STORY:

Wildlife photographer Joel Pastore shoots for *National Geographic* magazine, and specialises in taking pictures of endangered species, such as red wolves and ocelots. 'It's a matter of life and death, quite literally,' says Joel, 'and so the race is on to save [these animals]. My job is to get the public to first become aware that these creatures exist, then get them to care.'

DOWNLOADING YOUR PICTURES

Once you are happy with your snaps, it is time to transfer them to a computer. Downloading your pictures onto a computer is simple. Just connect your camera device to your computer and follow the instructions that came with your camera or phone.

Right way up Once your pictures are on the computer, they might show up sideways or upside down. To turn them all upright, find the rotate command in your photo viewer program and turn them clockwise or anti-clockwise. Whatever program you are using, you can find help by watching online video tutorials or by using your computer's help menu.

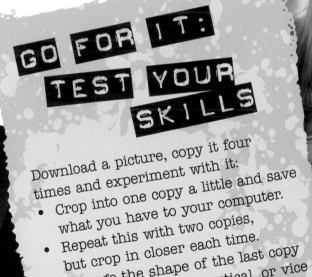

GO FOR IT: TEST YOUR SKILLS

Download a picture, copy it four times and experiment with it:
- Crop into one copy a little and save what you have to your computer.
- Repeat this with two copies, but crop in closer each time.
- Change the shape of the last copy from horizontal to vertical, or vice versa – which one looks best?

Downloading your pictures onto a computer is the first step to editing and improving your shots.

INSIDE STORY: PHOTO SHARING

In 2010, 26.9 billion photo prints were made worldwide. Half of these were done at home on home printers. This huge number was dwarfed by the amount of shots shared online. Facebook, Photobucket and Flickr share 75 billion photos between them. Apparently, women share twice as many photos as men!

Picture perfect Cropping is one of the quickest ways to improve a photo. Trimming out unnecessary or distracting objects in the background will draw people's attention to the main subject. Get rid of any red-eye with a photo-editing program such as PhotoSuite or Photoscape – both are free to download from the internet and will help to sort out your pictures in seconds.

Try it out Play around with brightness and contrast. Brightness lightens or darkens the shot. Contrast makes the shadows darker and the bright bits brighter. Increasing the contrast can improve the focus on a slightly blurred picture.

Lots of mobile phones allow you to share your shots on Facebook and Twitter as soon as you've taken them!

SERIOUS WITH SOFTWARE

If you want to be more adventurous with your shots, programs such as PhotoSuite can help you change colours and even retouch your pictures.

Photo-editing programs allow you to switch your pictures between colour and black and white.

Colouring a picture

Dodge and burn sound like something you would do in a computer game, but they are just better versions of brightness and contrast (see page 25). You can dodge a face to lighten it, or burn a background object to make it darker and less distracting. Most programs have tools to make black and white, sepia or saturated versions of your favourite shots – you just need to use the help menu or watch an online tutorial to find out how to do this.

GO FOR IT: DODGE AND BURN

Experiment with one of your photographs. First, decide which parts of the picture you want to draw attention to and which parts you would like to hide. Then follow these steps:

- To darken your background, choose the burn tool and to lighten your subject, choose the dodge tool.
- You will be shown a selection of virtual brushes – like paint brushes. Choose a fine brush to avoid mistakes.
- Select the 'strength' level – from 10 per cent to 100 per cent. Use a lower strength and go over a picture gradually rather than all at once. Your changes will blend in better.
- Once you have finished, save the file.

Need to retouch? You have taken a shot of your best friend but forgot about the background, and there is a tree 'growing' out of the top of their head. Do not worry. You can improve, or 'retouch' the picture using the stamp or clone tool. The idea is you copy a part of the picture – say a few millimetres of sky – and 'stamp' it down on top of the thing you want to get rid of. Repeat the process until it is all gone.

To improve the colours or alter the brightness in your pictures, experiment with the dodge and burn tools.

With a little practice, you'll be removing unwanted objects – like this telegraph pole – with ease!

EARLY DAYS: The magic touch

French retoucher Christophe Huet started out working in a printers and discovered that by retouching photographs he could turn them into works of art. He is famous today for his incredible photographs that are digitally retouched or distorted to create striking images such as people with enormous heads or people sinking into the ground.

STEP UP A GEAR

Now that you are taking great pictures, there are plenty of ways you can keep improving and enjoying your photography.

Add words to your pictures

Programs such as PhotoSuite allow you to add text to pictures, like putting 'Best Friends Forever' on a shot of your school friends. Follow the online instructions to see how this is done, and how to change the size of the words and the font used.

Share with friends

Sharing pictures is great fun. However, emailing high-resolution pictures can take a long time, and can clog up email inboxes. Instead, why not upload your pictures to a photo-sharing website such as snapfish, picasa or photobucket? Then you can send your friends the password for your gallery.

Networking

Another way to share your photos is to put them on a social networking site (such as Facebook), or to use a specialised photo-sharing site (such as Flickr). Have a look at these websites (ask permission if necessary) and work out how to put your shots online. Not only can you show people what great photos you have been taking, but by looking at other people's shots, you can also get some great ideas and inspiration.

If you really want to keep improving, read up on your subject and listen to the advice of experienced photographers. Happy snapping!

Merry Christmas

You can turn your photos into posters or even Christmas cards with the help of editing programs such as PhotoSuite.

Competition time! There are several 'Young Photographer of the Year' contests. Find out what is out there, send in your pictures and see how you do!

Talk to the pros Read up on your subject and talk to other photographers. You can get some great tips from the professionals that will save you loads of time messing about and making your own mistakes.

Build your own blog Why not create your own online blog? Go to a blog host such as Google's Blogger, Tumblr or WordPress, choose your site name, and follow the instructions to build a simple blog. You can include all your favourite pictures and even create different galleries for friends, family, holidays and school events.

GLOSSARY

apps short for applications – specialised computer programs designed to create different photographic effects on your camera phone

autofocus when a camera automatically focuses on what it thinks is the subject of your picture

burn a computer command that darkens a background object to make it less distracting

composition a way of describing how a picture is arranged, for example where someone is standing and how much sky is showing

cropping a way of cutting-out boring or unnecessary parts of a picture

depth of field the distance between the nearest and furthest objects that are in focus in a picture

dodge a computer command that can lighten specific parts of a picture to make them more eye-catching

downloading transferring pictures from your camera to a computer

enlarge to make something bigger

film a thin strip of plastic that reacts with light to produce images. Traditional cameras used film

flash a bright light that quickly goes on and off to brighten a picture

frame to compose an image to give the best possible result

imaginary something that is not really there

landscape a picture of an area of land, including all the important features of the area

maximise to make the best use of something

panning 'following' the subject of your photo with a camera to get sharper images of a moving subject

perseverance to keep doing something despite difficulties or delays

pixel a tiny part of an image that produces a full picture when it's combined with other pixels

red-eye an effect on pictures that occurs when the flash makes people look like they have red eyes

resolution a way of measuring how many pixels make up a full image

retouch to change an image by adding colour, or removing unwanted objects, for example

rotate to turn

saturated very bright and intensely-coloured

sepia a reddish-brown colour, usually seen on old photographs from the late-nineteenth century

shutter a tiny device on a camera that opens and shuts to let light in when you take a photograph

shutter speed the speed at which a shutter opens and closes

SLR short for single-lens reflex

still life a photograph of objects, usually showing a number of different textures

subject the person or thing that is the main image in your photograph

tripod a three-legged stand used to hold a camera steady

tweeted sent a message through the social media website Twitter

viewfinder the screen on the back of a digital camera that shows the image you have just taken or are about to take

zoom a type of lens that lets you take a much closer picture of your subject without having to move closer yourself

FURTHER INFORMATION

Books

Digital Photo Madness! by Thom Gaines
(Lark Books, 2010)

*How to Photograph Absolutely Everything:
Successful Pictures from your Digital Camera*
by Tom Ang (Dorling Kindersley, 2009)

The Kids' Guide to Digital Photography
by Jenni Bidner (Sterling, 2011)

Photography for Kids!
by Michael Ebert and Sandra Abend
(Rocky Nook, 2011)

*Really, Really, Really Easy Step-by-Step
Digital Photography* by Gavin Hoole
(New Holland Publishers, 2006)

Websites

Digital Photography School
Discover some great tips for all
levels of photographer
www.digital-photography-school.com

Digital Photographer
Amazing photo galleries and useful tutorials
for all ages
www.dphotographer.co.uk

Digital Photography
Advice on buying the right camera,
and lots of useful tips
www.digitalphotography.co.uk

EPhotozine
Interactive galleries where you can upload
your own photos for advice and comment
from other enthusiasts
www. ephotozine.com

Pro Photo Insights
Loads of useful video tutorials
– sign-up for free!
www.prophotoinsights.net

Photo Answers Online
Great advice and useful product reviews
from *Practical Photography* and *Digital Photo*
magazines
www. photoanswers.co.uk

Apps

Camera+
With over 3 million copies sold, this app
'supercharges' the standard camera on
your iPhone or iPod Touch and gives results
worthy of an SLR.

ColorSplash
This app lets you switch images into black
and white, keeping certain parts of the
picture in colour. Great fun for your iPhone,
iPod and iPad.

Hipstamatic
Discover great, old-fashioned looking pictures
for your iPhone or iPod Touch.

Photosynth
This app creates 360° shots by sticking
together individual photos you have taken!
If you want to capture a great mountain view,
or a picture of all your classmates at the
same time, this is the app for you.

INDEX

SERIES CONTENTS

Make A Film! Find your talent!
• What sort of film? • Create a script
• Make a shot list • Casting actors
• Location, location! • The right look
• And action! • Sound and lighting
• The shoot • All in the edit • Find
an audience • Step up a gear

Make A Podcast! Find your
talent! • The podcast story
• What's your big idea? • Get the
gear • Perfect planning • Start
recording • Credit to the edit
• From show to series • Going live
• Spread the word! • Guest stars
• Vodcast dreams • Step up a gear

Make An Animation! Find your
talent! • Moving pictures • The
basics • Classical style • Junk yard
• Make your own • Cut it out
• Story time • Shoot and load
• Picture perfect • Computer magic
• Sound it out • Step up a gear

Start A Band! Find your talent!
• Find your inspiration • Who do
you think you are? • Bandmates
wanted! • Band basics • Sort the
sessions • Go your own way
• Write a hit • Going live • Get
the gig • Room for improvement
• Do a demo • Step up a gear

Start A Blog! Find your talent!
• Welcome to the blogosphere!
• Blogging for beginners • What's
the plan? • Start it up • What is it
all about? • Get the look • Find your
voice • Picture perfect • Make it
multimedia! • We have lift-off!
• Going social • Step up a gear

Take Great Photos! Find your
talent! • Pick the moment • Taking
great photos • Sharp and clear
• Light it up • Still got it! • Say
cheese! • Fine-tuning your
portraits • Action shots • Playing
with animals • Downloading your
pictures • Serious with software
• Step up a gear